Cookie Count!

by Erin Sullivan

Table of Contents

What Do You Need to Make Your Cookies?

Your school is building a new library, and your class wants to help. What can a group of kids do to make some extra money?

You have a great idea: a **bake sale**! A bake sale involves a group of people making treats, such as brownies or cookies, and selling them. Your class decides to have a bake sale and give the money to your school library.

Did You Know?

In some countries, sprinkles are known as hundreds and thousands.

Brownies 75¢ each

2 cupcakes 50¢

Cakes $1.00 a slice

cookies 50¢ each

$1.00

You decide to make some sugar cookies for the bake sale. You find a **recipe**. But how many cookies should you make? Most people make cookies by the **dozen**. A dozen is a group of twelve. How many cookies would you have if you made two dozen? Three dozen? Four dozen?

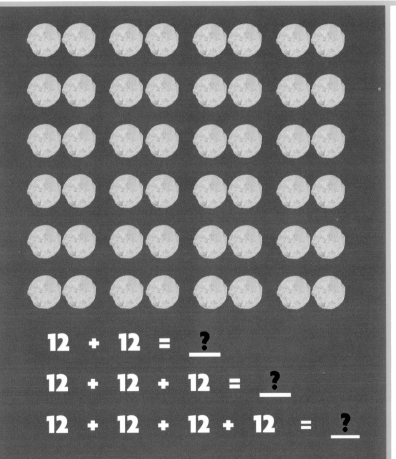

12 + 12 = ?

12 + 12 + 12 = ?

12 + 12 + 12 + 12 = ?

+ 🍪 = a baker's dozen

The term "baker's dozen" actually means 13, not 12! A legend says that an evil spell was placed on a greedy baker who would not give an extra roll to a poor old woman. The spell could not be broken until he gave her 13 rolls in all, or a baker's dozen.

You're off to the store! It's time to buy the ingredients for your cookie recipe. You'll need to buy flour, butter, sugar, and eggs.

Weighing It Up!

If you look closely at the packages, you'll see that each item weighs a different amount. The eggs are sold in cartons. Each carton contains a dozen or half a dozen eggs.

▲ Amount: 1 dozen

▲ Weight: 3 pounds

▲ Weight: 1 pound

▲ Weight: 4 pounds

◉Did You Know?

There are 16 ounces in one pound.

4

The store is having a **sale**! Each price tag shows the regular price of the item. Each tag also shows the sale price. You can figure out how much you save by subtracting the sale price from the regular price. How much will you save on each item?

S A L E !
Regular Price ~~$3.00~~
Sale Price – $ 2.00
You Save = $ ___

S A L E !
Regular Price ~~$2.50~~
Sale Price – $ 2.00
You Save = $ ___

S A L E !
Regular Price ~~$4.00~~
Sale Price – $ 2.00
You Save = $ ___

S A L E !
Regular Price ~~$1.50~~
Sale Price – $ 1.25
You Save = $ ___

Bar Codes

9 379674 210649

A bar code is made up of numbers and stripes. When a bar code gets scanned at the checkout, the price of the item comes up on the cash register.

5

You've got your ingredients. Now you need your cooking tools. You go to the kitchen to find a bowl, a mixing spoon, a cookie tray, a set of measuring spoons, and a set of measuring cups.

Look at the measuring cups closely. How much can each one hold? How many $\frac{1}{8}$ cups of flour does it take to fill the 1-cup measure? How many $\frac{1}{4}$ cups of flour does it take to fill the 1-cup measure? How many $\frac{1}{2}$ cups of flour does it take to fill the 1-cup measure?

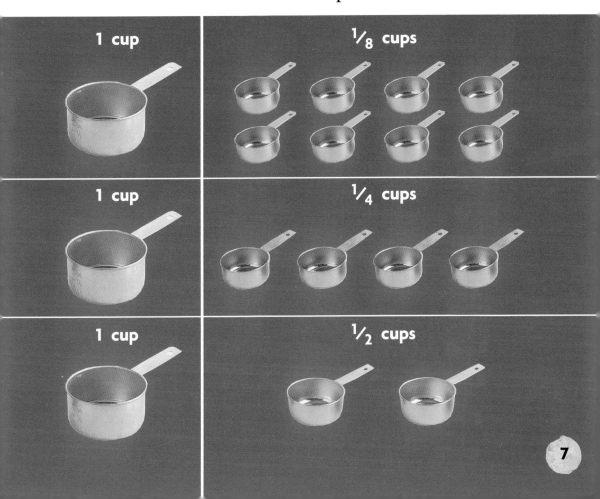

1 cup

$\frac{1}{8}$ cups

1 cup

$\frac{1}{4}$ cups

1 cup

$\frac{1}{2}$ cups

How Do You Use Math to Make Your Cookies?

It's time to read the recipe carefully! Look at the information the recipe gives. At the top, you see the title and the number of cookies the recipe makes. Then you see the list of ingredients along with the amount of each ingredient needed. At the bottom, you see the step-by-step directions for making your cookies.

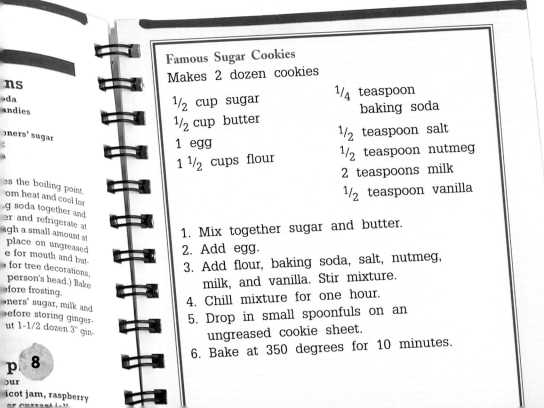

Famous Sugar Cookies
Makes 2 dozen cookies

$1/2$ cup sugar
$1/2$ cup butter
1 egg
1 $1/2$ cups flour

$1/4$ teaspoon baking soda
$1/2$ teaspoon salt
$1/2$ teaspoon nutmeg
2 teaspoons milk
$1/2$ teaspoon vanilla

1. Mix together sugar and butter.
2. Add egg.
3. Add flour, baking soda, salt, nutmeg, milk, and vanilla. Stir mixture.
4. Chill mixture for one hour.
5. Drop in small spoonfuls on an ungreased cookie sheet.
6. Bake at 350 degrees for 10 minutes.

You have decided to make 4 dozen, or 48, cookies. The recipe makes only 2 dozen, or 24, cookies. That means you will need to double the recipe. You need twice as much of each ingredient. For example, the recipe asks for $\frac{1}{2}$ cup of sugar.

$\frac{1}{2}$ **cup sugar +** $\frac{1}{2}$ **cup sugar = 1 cup sugar**

Can you double the rest of the ingredients?

DOUBLING THE RECIPE

$\frac{1}{2}$ cup butter	**+**	$\frac{1}{2}$ cup butter	**=**	**?**
1 egg	**+**	1 egg	**=**	**?**
$1\frac{1}{2}$ cups flour	**+**	$1\frac{1}{2}$ cups flour	**=**	**?**

You follow the recipe's directions, step by step. Soon you have a tasty-looking cookie dough. Now it's time to lay out your cookies on the cookie tray. You can fit 4 rows of cookies on each tray, with 3 cookies in each row. How many cookies will there be on the tray?

$$\begin{array}{r} 3 \\ + \ 3 \\ + \ 3 \\ + \ 3 \\ \hline ? \end{array}$$

Remember that you are making 4 dozen, or 48, cookies. You can fit only 12 cookies on the tray. How many trays will you need to cook the whole batch?

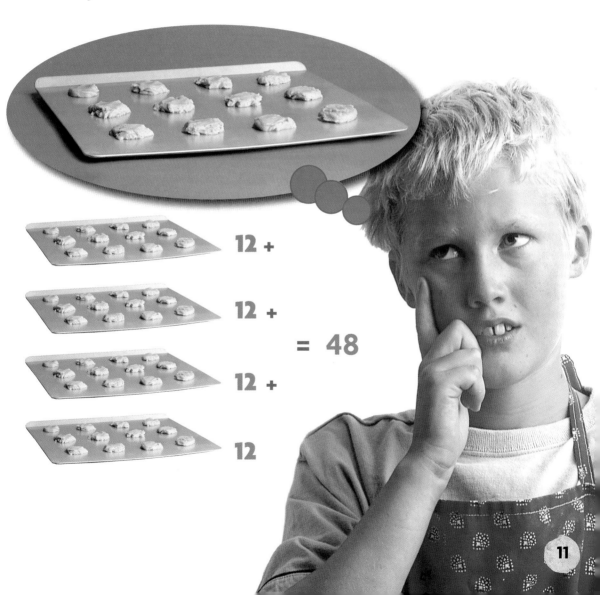

12 +

12 +

= 48

12 +

12

How Do You Bake Your Cookies?

Your cookies are ready to bake. The recipe says to set the oven to 350 degrees. Many cookies bake at this **temperature**.

Baked Ice Cream?

Can you cook ice cream without melting it? Yes! Some chefs make a fancy dessert called Baked Alaska, in which they create a "mountain" of ice cream, cover it with a whipped egg mixture, and bake it in a very hot oven for three minutes. It's hot and cold—and delicious—at the same time!

If you look at your oven dial, you will probably see numbers that go from about 250 degrees to about 450 degrees. Some foods need to cook at low temperatures for a long time, while other foods need to cook at high temperatures for a short time.

Here are the temperatures at which some other foods cook.

▶ roast beef
275 degrees

▶ banana bread
375 degrees

▶ apple pie
400 degrees

▶ baked potato
425 degrees

If you look at the recipe, you will see that one tray of cookies takes 10 minutes to bake. How long will it take to bake all of your cookies?

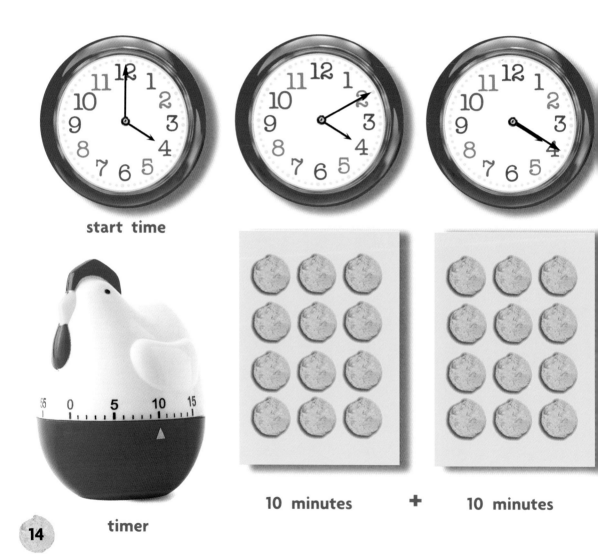

start time

10 minutes + 10 minutes

timer

Now think about when you will be done baking all of the cookies. If you start at 4:00 P.M., and you bake one tray of cookies at a time, at what time will you finish?

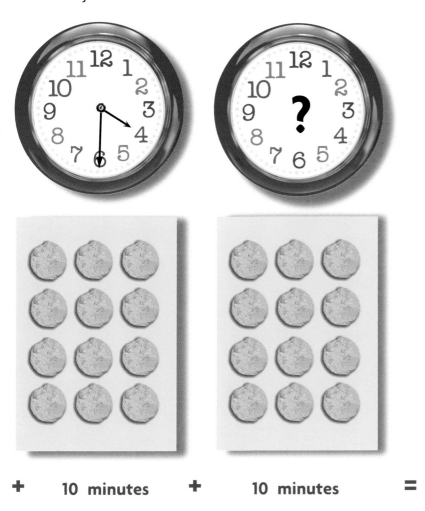

\+ **10 minutes** \+ **10 minutes** = **?**

How Do You Decorate Your Cookies?

Your cookies look great! They are ready to be decorated. You make some frosting and decide how you want to decorate the cookies.

You want to make designs and patterns that are **symmetrical**. This means that the design on one half of the cookie is the same as the design on the other half.

Fun with Frosting

You can make this frosting to decorate your cookies.

You will need:
- 1 ½ ounces butter
- 2 teaspoons milk
- 1 cup confectioners' sugar
- 3 drops of food coloring of your choice

1. Ask an adult to put the butter in a microwave-safe bowl and cook it for a few seconds on High.

2. Stir in the milk and confectioners' sugar. The mixture should not be runny.

3. Add food coloring.

Run, Run, As Fast As You Can . . .

The famous gingerbread man was invented about 450 years ago at the court of Queen Elizabeth I of England. Bakers designed cookies in the shape of people to look like friends of the queen.

A symmetrical design has a **line of symmetry**. This is an imaginary line that you can draw through the middle of the design, so that each half looks exactly the same.

Look at these decorated cookies. Try to find two cookies with symmetrical designs. When you find them, find the line of symmetry on each one.

How Much Money Will Your Bake Sale Make?

It's time for the bake sale. You decide to sell your cookies for 50 cents each. How much money will you make if you sell 2 cookies?

$$50¢ + 50¢ = ?$$

How much money will you make if you sell 8 cookies?

$$50¢ + 50¢ + 50¢ + 50¢ + 50¢ + 50¢ + 50¢ + 50¢ = ?$$

$$50¢ + 50¢ + 50¢ + 50¢ + 50¢ + 50¢ + 50¢ + 50¢ + 50¢ + 50¢ = ?$$

How much money will you make if you sell 10 cookies?

Can you figure out how much money you will make if you sell all 48 cookies?

Congratulations! Your bake sale was a success!

Cookie Count! Answers

Page 3   24 cookies in 2 dozen;
36 cookies in 3 dozen;
48 cookies in 4 dozen

Page 5   Flour: $3.00 − $2.00 = $1.00;
Butter: $2.50 − $2.00 = $ 0.50;
Sugar: $4.00 − $2.00 = $2.00;
Eggs: $1.50 − $1.25 = $ 0.25

Page 7   Eight $^1/_8$ cups in 1 cup;
four $^1/_4$ cups in 1 cup; two $^1/_2$ cups in 1 cup

Page 9   1 cup butter, 2 eggs, 3 cups flour,
$^1/_2$ teaspoon baking soda, 1 teaspoon salt,
1 teaspoon nutmeg, 4 teaspoons milk,
1 teaspoon vanilla

Page 10 12 cookies on each tray

Page 11 4 trays needed for 48 cookies

Pages 14–15 Cookies will take 40 minutes to bake.
The baking will be done at 4:40 P.M.

Page 17 Cookies A and C are the most symmetrical.
Cookies D, E, and F would be symmetrical if
the sprinkles on each half were identical in color
and position. Cookie B is not symmetrical.

Page 18 2 cookies = $1.00; 8 cookies = $4.00;
10 cookies = $5.00; 48 cookies = $24.00

Glossary

bake sale (BAKE SALE): selling homemade treats, such as brownies or cookies, for a good cause

dozen (DUH-zen): a group of twelve

line of symmetry (LINE UV SIH-meh-tree): the imaginary line that divides a symmetrical design in half so that it is identical on both halves

recipe (REH-sih-pee): directions for making a kind of food

sale (SALE): the act of selling an item for less than it usually costs

symmetrical (sih-MEH-trih-kul): when a design is exactly the same on each half

temperature (TEM-puh-ruh-cher): the measurement of heat

Index